Wildlife that Hides

By Clem King

Lots of wildlife have tricks to help them hide.

Can you see the wildlife?

Can you see wildlife on this page?

The stonefish's skin
looks like its habitat.

You could mistake it for a rock!

You could mistake this
for just moss.
But some of it is **not** moss!

That page includes a frog!

The frog's bumpy skin
helps it hide in the moss.

Can you see wildlife on this page?

If not, I suppose you have a great excuse.

Look again at the branch.

Do you see the outline of a gecko now?

This fox's grey fur blends into its habitat.

But sometimes, its habitat is all white.

When the landscape gets cold and snowy, the fox makes its fur white to match.

An octopus can update the shade of its skin to match its habitat.

If something hunts the octopus,
it updates its shade.
Then it hides and escapes.

Likewise, this reptile can update its shade to match the landscape.

This female reptile wants to be left alone.

But this male reptile updates its skin to bright shades to find a friend!

Sometimes, animals hide by mistake.

Where is my cat?

CHECKING FOR MEANING

1. What does the skin of the stonefish look like? *(Literal)*
2. What does the fox do when its habitat becomes cold and snowy? *(Literal)*
3. Why do animals try to match their habitat? *(Inferential)*
4. Do you think these hiding tricks work for the wildlife? Why? *(Evaluative)*

EXTENDING VOCABULARY

habitat	What is a habitat? What are some examples of animals' habitats?
mistake	The word *mistake* can be a noun or a verb. In the sentence *You could mistake it for a rock!* what part of speech is the word *mistake*?
outline	What are the two smaller words that make up the word *outline*? How do they help you understand the meaning of the whole word?

MOVING BEYOND THE TEXT

1. When animals change their fur or skin to match their habitats, they are using "camouflage". What other animals do you know that use camouflage to hide?
2. When an animal is using camouflage, how might a predator use its other senses to help it find the hidden animal?
3. The reptile on page 12 is a chameleon. Chameleons sometimes use different skin colours to stand out and catch the attention of their friends. What other animals use colours to stand out? Why do they want to stand out?
4. What other reptiles do you know? What are some differences between reptiles and mammals?

TIME TO WRITE

Imagine you are an animal that needs to hide. Write about what you look like before you hide and then describe what tricks you use to match your habitat.